Jr. Graphic Colonial America

THE MYSTERY OF ROANOKE,
the Lost Colony

Andrea P. Smith

PowerKiDS press.

Published in 2012 by The Rosen Publishing Group, Inc.
29 East 21st Street, New York, NY 10010

First Edition

Editor: Joanne Randolph
Book Design: Planman Technologies
Illustrations: Planman Technologies

Library of Congress Cataloging-in-Publication Data

Smith, Andrea P.
  The mystery of Roanoke, the Lost Colony / by Andrea P. Smith. — 1st ed.
      p. cm. — (Jr. graphic Colonial America)
  Includes index.
  ISBN 978-1-4488-5185-0 (library binding) — ISBN 978-1-4488-5208-6 (pbk.) —
  ISBN 978-1-4488-5209-3 (6-pack)
  1. Roanoke Colony—Juvenile literature. 2. Roanoke Island (N.C.)—History—
  16th century—Juvenile literature. 3. Roanoke Colony—Comic books, strips, etc.
  4. Roanoke Island (N.C.)—History—16th century—Comic books, strips, etc.
  I. Title.
  F229.S56 2012
  975.6'175—dc22
                                                                    2011001703

Manufactured in the United States of America

CPSIA Compliance Information: Batch #PLS1102PK: For Further Information contact Rosen Publishing, New York, New York at 1-800-237-9932

CONTENTS

MAIN CHARACTERS

John White (1540?–1593) An English artist and explorer. White led the second **expedition** of **settlers** to Roanoke and started the first English **colony** in the Americas. He became governor of Roanoke Colony.

Ananias Dare (1560?–1587?) and **Eleanor Dare (1563–1599?)** Ananias Dare had been a bricklayer in London, England, and was part of the second Roanoke expedition. His wife, Eleanor, was John White's daughter.

Virginia Dare (August 18, 1587–?) The first English child born in the New World. Her parents were Ananias and Eleanor Dare. Her grandfather was John White.

Manteo (c. 1500s) A Croatan Native American who was born on Roanoke Island. He helped Ralph Lane and his colonists survive their first winter at Roanoke. He traveled to England with Sir Walter Raleigh, where he learned English. Manteo returned to Roanoke and served as an **interpreter** for the English colonists.

Wingina (c. 1500s) The chief of the Roanoke Island tribe of Native Americans. He helped the colonists survive at Roanoke and was later killed by English colonists.

The Mystery of Roanoke, the Lost Colony

AUGUST 1590. JOHN WHITE NEARS ROANOKE ISLAND, WHERE HE HAD LEFT SETTLERS THREE YEARS BEFORE.

HOPE WELL

I'VE WAITED THREE LONG YEARS TO RETURN. WHAT WILL WE FIND?

THE MEN BOARDED ROWBOATS AND STARTED OUT FOR CAPE HATTERAS TO BEGIN THEIR **SEARCH**.

LET'S HURRY. I WANT TO FIND MY DAUGHTER, ELEANOR, AND MY GRANDDAUGHTER, VIRGINIA.

ONE ROWBOAT **CAPSIZED**, AND SOME OF THE MEN DROWNED. WHEN THE MEN FINALLY REACHED THE SHORE, THEY COULD NOT FIND ANY OF THE COLONISTS.

JOHN WHITE AND HIS MEN SAILED ALONG THE COAST LOOKING FOR SIGNS OF LIFE.

LOOK, MEN, A FIRE! MAYBE THE COLONISTS ARE COOKING FOOD.

THEY WERE DISAPPOINTED NOT TO FIND PEOPLE. THE WILDFIRE HAD DIED DOWN.

HAS SOMEONE TRIED TO LEAVE A MESSAGE?

CROATOAN IS A NEARBY ISLAND. PERHAPS THE SETTLERS HAVE MOVED.

WHAT HAS HAPPENED HERE? EVERYONE'S GONE.

IT LOOKS SO PEACEFUL. DID EVERYONE DECIDE TO MOVE AWAY?

WE SEARCHED ALONG THE CREEK AND FOUND NO SIGNS OF THEM.

JOHN WHITE SAW HIS **ARMOR** AMONG WHAT WAS LEFT BEHIND. HE COULD ONLY GUESS WHERE THE SETTLERS WERE, THOUGH. WERE THEY STILL ALIVE? COULD HE FIND THEM?

NEEDING FRESH FOOD AND WATER, THE CAPTAIN SET SAIL FOR TRINIDAD. JOHN WHITE FAILED TO FIND THE SETTLERS.

THREE YEARS EARLIER. . .

RALPH LANE ALREADY FAILED ON ROANOKE ISLAND, AND HE MADE ENEMIES AMONG THE NATIVES.

LANE FAILED FOR MANY REASONS. I PLAN TO TAKE MEN, WOMEN, AND CHILDREN TO FORM A REAL **COMMUNITY**.

I BELIEVE IT IS A GOOD PLACE TO MAKE A **PERMANENT** SETTLEMENT FOR THE ENGLISH.

CERTAINLY A PLACE WITH A GOOD HARBOR WOULD BE BETTER.

THE TWO MEN AGREED ON A PLACE ON CHESAPEAKE BAY. WHITE OFFERED 500 ACRES (202 HA) OF FARMLAND TO EACH HEAD OF A HOUSEHOLD, A GOOD REASON FOR PEOPLE TO TAKE THE CHANCE.

MAY 8, 1587.

LION

THE COLONISTS SET SAIL FOR THEIR NEW LIFE.

HAVE YOU SEEN SIMON FERNANDEZ, OUR PILOT? HE IS LETTING ONE SHIP FALL FAR BEHIND THE OTHERS.

TWO SHIPS REACHED ROANOKE ISLAND, AND THE COLONISTS WENT ASHORE. THEY HOPED TO FIND THE 15 MEN LANE LEFT BEHIND WHEN HE LEFT.

MY SHIPS ARE LEAVING. WE HAVE SPANISH SHIPS TO RAID.

MUCH TO THEIR SURPRISE, THE COLONISTS WOULD NOT BE SETTLING ON CHESAPEAKE BAY. THEY WERE LEFT ON ROANOKE ISLAND.

THE COLONISTS DID NOT FIND LANE'S MEN. ONE SKELETON AND A RAIDED FORT WERE ALL THE COLONISTS FOUND.

THE COLONISTS HAD FEW CHOICES. THEY REBUILT THE FORT AND SET TO WORK ON BUILDING THEIR HOMES.

I DIDN'T THINK WE WOULD EVER SEE THEM AGAIN. NOW OUR COLONY WILL BE COMPLETE.

THE THIRD SHIP REACHED ROANOKE ISLAND AT LAST.

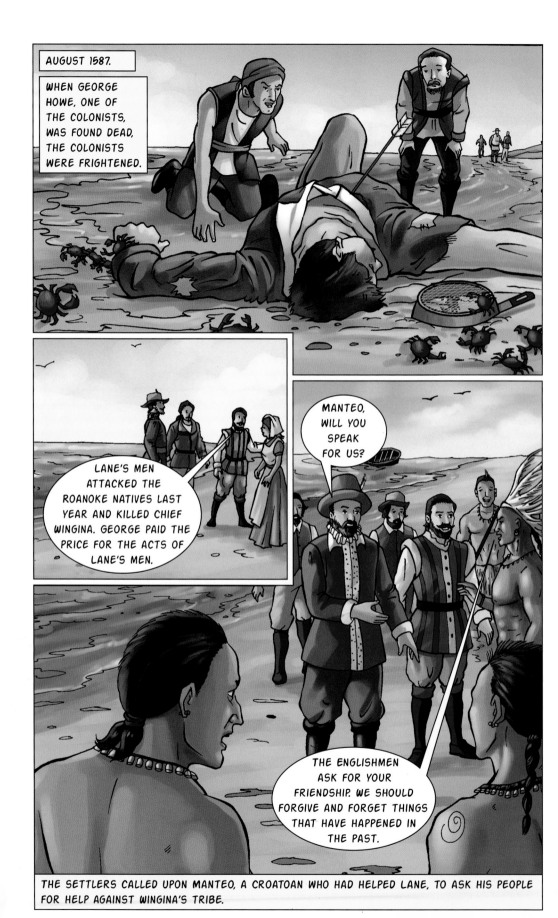

AUGUST 1587.

WHEN GEORGE HOWE, ONE OF THE COLONISTS, WAS FOUND DEAD, THE COLONISTS WERE FRIGHTENED.

LANE'S MEN ATTACKED THE ROANOKE NATIVES LAST YEAR AND KILLED CHIEF WINGINA. GEORGE PAID THE PRICE FOR THE ACTS OF LANE'S MEN.

MANTEO, WILL YOU SPEAK FOR US?

THE ENGLISHMEN ASK FOR YOUR FRIENDSHIP. WE SHOULD FORGIVE AND FORGET THINGS THAT HAVE HAPPENED IN THE PAST.

THE SETTLERS CALLED UPON MANTEO, A CROATOAN WHO HAD HELPED LANE, TO ASK HIS PEOPLE FOR HELP AGAINST WINGINA'S TRIBE.

THE COLONISTS RETURNED TO ROANOKE AND WAITED FOR AN ANSWER.

WE WAIT NO LONGER. WE WILL ATTACK WINGINA'S MEN. WITHOUT AN OFFER OF PEACE, OTHERS WILL DIE.

WHITE PLANNED TO KILL ONE OF WINGINA'S ROANOKE INDIANS. HIS MEN KILLED ONE OF THE FRIENDLY CROATANS INSTEAD.

WAS THEIR CHANCE FOR PEACE GONE?

MANTEO EXPLAINED THE MISTAKE TO HIS PEOPLE. THE COLONISTS WERE THANKFUL THAT MANTEO GOT A PEACE AGREEMENT.

13

ON AUGUST 18, 1587, JOHN WHITE'S DAUGHTER, ELEANOR DARE, GAVE BIRTH TO A DAUGHTER, VIRGINIA DARE.

CONGRATULATIONS, ANANIAS! YOUR BEAUTIFUL BABY, VIRGINIA, IS THE FIRST ENGLISH PERSON BORN IN THE NEW WORLD.

OUR SUPPLIES ARE RUNNING LOW. WE NEED SHIPMENTS FROM HOME. PLEASE GO TO ENGLAND TO GET WHAT WE NEED.

I CAN'T LEAVE YOU. THERE ARE TOO MANY DECISIONS TO BE MADE.

THE COLONISTS PERSUADED WHITE TO RETURN TO ENGLAND. HE WAS TO BRING BACK MUCH-NEEDED SUPPLIES.

JOHN WHITE LEFT THE COLONISTS.

APRIL–MAY 1588.

UPON HIS RETURN HOME, WHITE MET WITH RALEIGH.

WE WERE LEFT ON ROANOKE ISLAND. OUR PLANS TO MOVE TO CHESAPEAKE BAY ARE ON HOLD. FIRST WE NEED SUPPLY SHIPMENTS.

SIR WALTER RALEIGH FINALLY AGREED TO GIVE WHITE TWO SMALL SHIPS. THEY WERE NOT NEEDED TO FIGHT THE SPANIARDS. WHITE PREPARED TO SET SAIL WITH THE SUPPLIES.

WHITE'S SHIPS WERE ATTACKED BY FRENCH SHIPS JUST AFTER HE SET SAIL. A BATTLE TOOK PLACE AND THE FRENCH WON.

WHITE WATCHED HELPLESSLY AS THE FRENCH STOLE ALL THE SUPPLIES. TWO MORE YEARS PASSED BEFORE WHITE COULD RETURN TO ROANOKE ISLAND.

WHEN WHITE FINALLY ARRIVED, HE FOUND ONE OF HISTORY'S GREAT UNSOLVED MYSTERIES. WHAT HAPPENED TO THE COLONISTS?

EVEN AFTER WHITE RETURNED TO ENGLAND ONCE AGAIN, THE COLONISTS WERE NOT FORGOTTEN. JAMESTOWN WAS SETTLED 120 MILES (193 KM) NORTH IN 1607. COLONISTS FROM JAMESTOWN SENT SEVERAL GROUPS TO LOOK FOR THE LOST COLONISTS.

DURING THE CIVIL WAR, UNION SOLDIERS DUG FOR **ARTIFACTS** ON ROANOKE ISLAND.

AXE FOUND ON ROANOKE ISLAND

THERE IS MORE THAN ONE **THEORY** ABOUT WHAT MAY HAVE HAPPENED TO THE LOST COLONY. SOME BELIEVE THE COLONISTS MOVED INLAND.

SOME BELIEVE THE CROATANS, WHO LIVED 50 MILES (80 KM) INLAND, TOOK THE COLONISTS INTO THEIR COMMUNITY.

OTHERS BELIEVE THE COLONISTS WERE KILLED BY NATIVE AMERICANS.

TODAY THE AREA WHERE THE LOST COLONY WAS IS **PROTECTED** AS PART OF FORT RALEIGH, A NATIONAL HISTORIC SITE.

SCIENTISTS HAVE LEARNED MORE ABOUT THE LOST COLONY THROUGH SITE **EXCAVATION**, SATELLITE IMAGING, AND EVEN DNA TESTING OF THE **DESCENDANTS** OF THE CROATAN INDIANS.

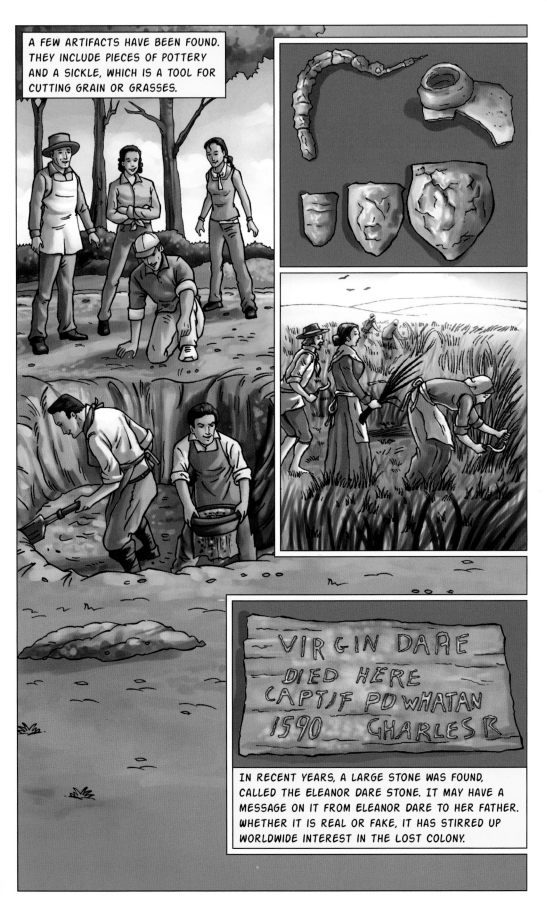

A FEW ARTIFACTS HAVE BEEN FOUND. THEY INCLUDE PIECES OF POTTERY AND A SICKLE, WHICH IS A TOOL FOR CUTTING GRAIN OR GRASSES.

VIRGIN DARE
DIED HERE
CAPT/F PDWHATAN
1590   CHARLES R

IN RECENT YEARS, A LARGE STONE WAS FOUND, CALLED THE ELEANOR DARE STONE. IT MAY HAVE A MESSAGE ON IT FROM ELEANOR DARE TO HER FATHER. WHETHER IT IS REAL OR FAKE, IT HAS STIRRED UP WORLDWIDE INTEREST IN THE LOST COLONY.

TIMELINE

March 1584   Queen Elizabeth grants Sir Walter Raleigh the right to plan settlements and start colonies in the New World. He sends two ships to search for a place to start an English colony.

August 1585   Roanoke is picked as the site for the first English settlement in the New World. Houses and a fort are built.

Winter 1585   Native Americans supply food for the settlers and help them survive the winter.

June 1586   Wingina, the Roanoke Native American chief, is believed to be uniting Native American tribes against the English. He is killed by the English settlers.

July 1586   The settlers return to England.

August 1586   Fifteen new settlers are left as caretakers on Roanoke. They are never heard from again.

May 1587   John White leaves England with 117 settlers to set up a new colony in the New World.

July 1587   White arrives at Roanoke Island with his group of settlers and begins rebuilding the houses.

August 1587   Virginia Dare is born. She is the first English person born in the New World.

August 1587   John White leaves Roanoke to travel to England so that he can bring supplies back to the colony.

August 1590   White finally returns to Roanoke. He finds no colonists and is forced to return to England.

April 1607   The English start a permanent settlement in Jamestown.

1998   Scientists learn through their study of tree ring growth of trees in North Carolina that the worst drought in 800 years happened at the time the English were trying to start a colony at Roanoke.

GLOSSARY

armor (AR-mer) A type of uniform used in battle to help protect the body.

artifacts (AR-tih-fakts) Objects made by people.

capsized (KAP-syzd) Became overturned.

colony (KAH-luh-nee) A new place where people move that is still ruled by the leaders of the country from which they came.

community (kuh-MYOO-nih-tee) A place where people live and work together or the people who make up such a place.

descendants (dih-SEN-dents) People who are born of a certain family or group.

excavation (ek-skuh-VAY-shun) Digging up things that were buried.

expedition (ek-spuh-DIH-shun) A trip for a special purpose.

interpreter (in-TER-prih-ter) Someone who helps people who speak different languages talk to each other.

permanent (PER-muh-nint) Lasting forever.

protected (pruh-TEKT-ed) Kept safe.

search (SERCH) To look for something.

settlers (SET-lerz) People who move to a new land to live.

theory (THEE-uh-ree) An idea or group of ideas that tries to explain something.

INDEX

A
Americas, 3
armor, 6
artifacts, 18, 21

C
Chesapeake Bay, 8, 10, 15
colonists, 10, 11, 12, 13, 15, 17, 18, 19
colony, 3, 11
Croatans, 3, 13, 19, 20
Croatoan, 6, 7

D
Dare, Ananias, 3, 14
Dare, Eleanor, 3, 4, 14, 21
Dare, Virginia, 3, 4, 14

E
England, 3, 14, 18

F
Fernandez, Simon, 9
fort, 6, 11
Fort Raleigh, 20

H
Hatteras, Cape, 4
Hopewell, 4, 5, 7
Howe, George, 12

J
Jamestown, 18

L
Lane, Ralph, 3, 8, 10, 11, 12
Lion, 9
Lost Colony, 19, 20

M
Manteo, 3, 12, 13

N
New World, 14

R
Raleigh, Walter, 3, 8, 13, 16
Roanoke, 3, 8, 10, 15, 17, 18
Roanoke tribe, 3, 12, 13

S
settlement, 8
settlers, 3, 6, 7

T
Trinidad, 7

W
White, John, 3, 7, 8, 14, 15, 16, 17, 18
Wingina, 3, 12, 13

WEB SITES

Due to the changing nature of Internet links, PowerKids Press has developed an online list of Web sites related to the subject of this book. This site is updated regularly. Please use this link to access the list:

www.powerkidslinks.com/JGCO/roanoke